World's Weirdest Plants

Dragon's Blood Trees Bleed!

By Janey Levy

Gareth Stevens Publishing

Please visit our website, www.garethstevens.com. For a free color catalog of all our high-quality books, call toll free 1-800-542-2595 or fax 1-877-542-2596.

Library of Congress Cataloging-in-Publication Data

Names: Levy, Janey, author.
Title: Dragon's blood trees bleed! / Janey Levy.
Description: New York : Gareth Stevens Publishing, [2020] | Series: World's weirdest plants | Includes index.
Identifiers: LCCN 2019030742 | ISBN 9781538246436 | ISBN 9781538246443 (library binding) | ISBN 9781538246429 (paperback) | ISBN 9781538246450 (ebook)
Subjects: LCSH: Dracaena–Juvenile literature.
Classification: LCC QK495.A83 L48 2020 | DDC 584/.79–dc23
LC record available at https://lccn.loc.gov/2019030742

First Edition

Published in 2020 by
Gareth Stevens Publishing
111 East 14th Street, Suite 349
New York, NY 10003

Designer: Katelyn E. Reynolds
Editor: Abby Badach Doyle

Photo credits: Cover, pp. 1, 11 Oleg Znamenskiy/Shutterstock.com; cover, pp. 1–24 (background) Conny Sjostrom/Shutterstock.com; cover, pp. 1–24 (sign elements) A Sk/Shutterstock.com; p. 5 sunsinger/Shutterstock.com; p. 7 Peter Hermes Furian/Shutterstock.com; p. 9 (tree graphic) Chalintra.B/Shutterstock.com; p. 9 (flowers) DEA / V. GIANNELLA/De Agostini/Getty Images; p. 9 (berries) ArliftAtoz2205/Shutterstock.com; pp. 9 (branches), 13 (main) Vladimir Melnik/Shutterstock.com; p. 13 (inset) Naeblys/Shutterstock.com; p. 15 Rhonda Gutenberg/Lonely Planet Images/Getty Images; p. 16 Andy Dingley/Wikipedia.org; p. 17 Sylvain CORDIER/Gamma-Rapho via Getty Images; p. 19 PATRICK KOVARIK/AFP/Getty Images; p. 21 Michail_Vorobyev/Shuttterstock.com.

Printed in the United States of America

CONTENTS

Words in the glossary appear in **bold** type the first time they are used in the text.

THE STRANGE DRAGON'S BLOOD TREE

"Dragon's blood" is a weird name for a tree, isn't it? You're likely wondering why in the world it's called that! Well, one tale says the first dragon's blood tree was created from the blood of a dragon that was hurt in a fight with an elephant.

But there's another reason, too. The strange-looking tree seems to bleed when it's hurt! The red liquid that comes out of it is known as dragon's blood. You'll learn all about this strange tree inside this book.

The dragon's blood tree is also sometimes called the Socotra dragon tree.

THE TREE'S TERRITORY

If you want to see the dragon's blood tree in its native home, you'll have to travel a long way. It grows on the tiny island of Socotra in the Indian Ocean. The island is part of the Republic of Yemen.

On the island, the tree grows in areas you might not expect to find trees. It grows on mountains made of hard stone called granite. It also grows on **plateaus** (pla-TOHZ) made of rock called limestone.

SEEDS OF KNOWLEDGE

The island of Socotra is a special place. It has over 800 kinds of plants, and over one-third of those are found nowhere else in the world.

Where Dragon's Blood Trees Live

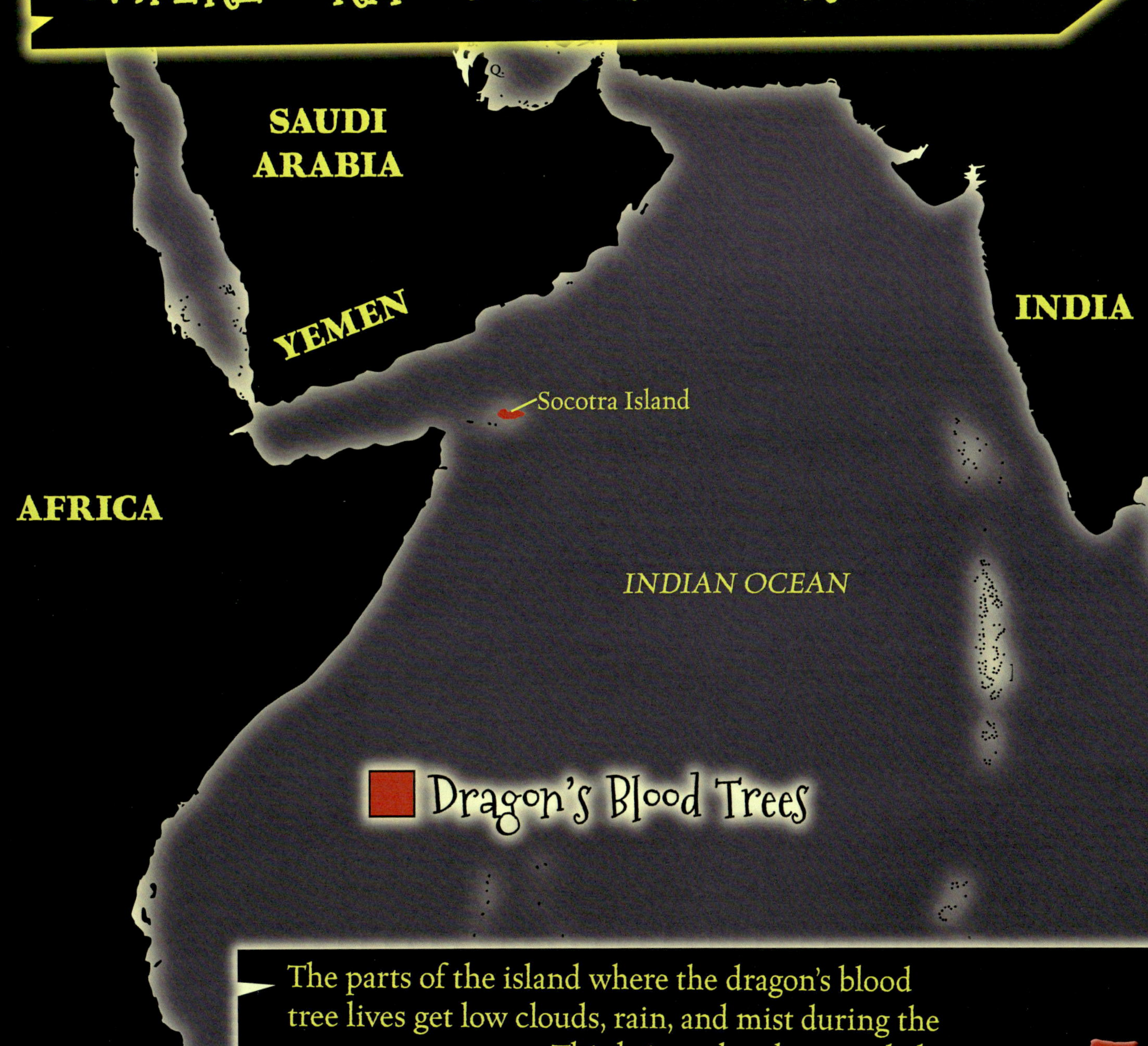

The parts of the island where the dragon's blood tree lives get low clouds, rain, and mist during the **monsoon** season. This brings the plant needed water.

HOW THEY GROW

Have you ever eaten an apple and seen the seeds inside it? Those seeds can grow new apple trees. Dragon's blood trees also grow from seeds. Those seeds grow into sturdy **trunks** from which branches grow.

Stiff, long leaves grow at the ends of the branches. In February, small white or green flowers appear at the ends of the branches. Those flowers produce green berries that ripen to orange-red. Birds and animals eat the berries and spread their seeds. Then, the **cycle** begins again.

SEEDS OF KNOWLEDGE

Dragon's blood trees can live for up to 1,000 years!

The Dragon's Blood Tree

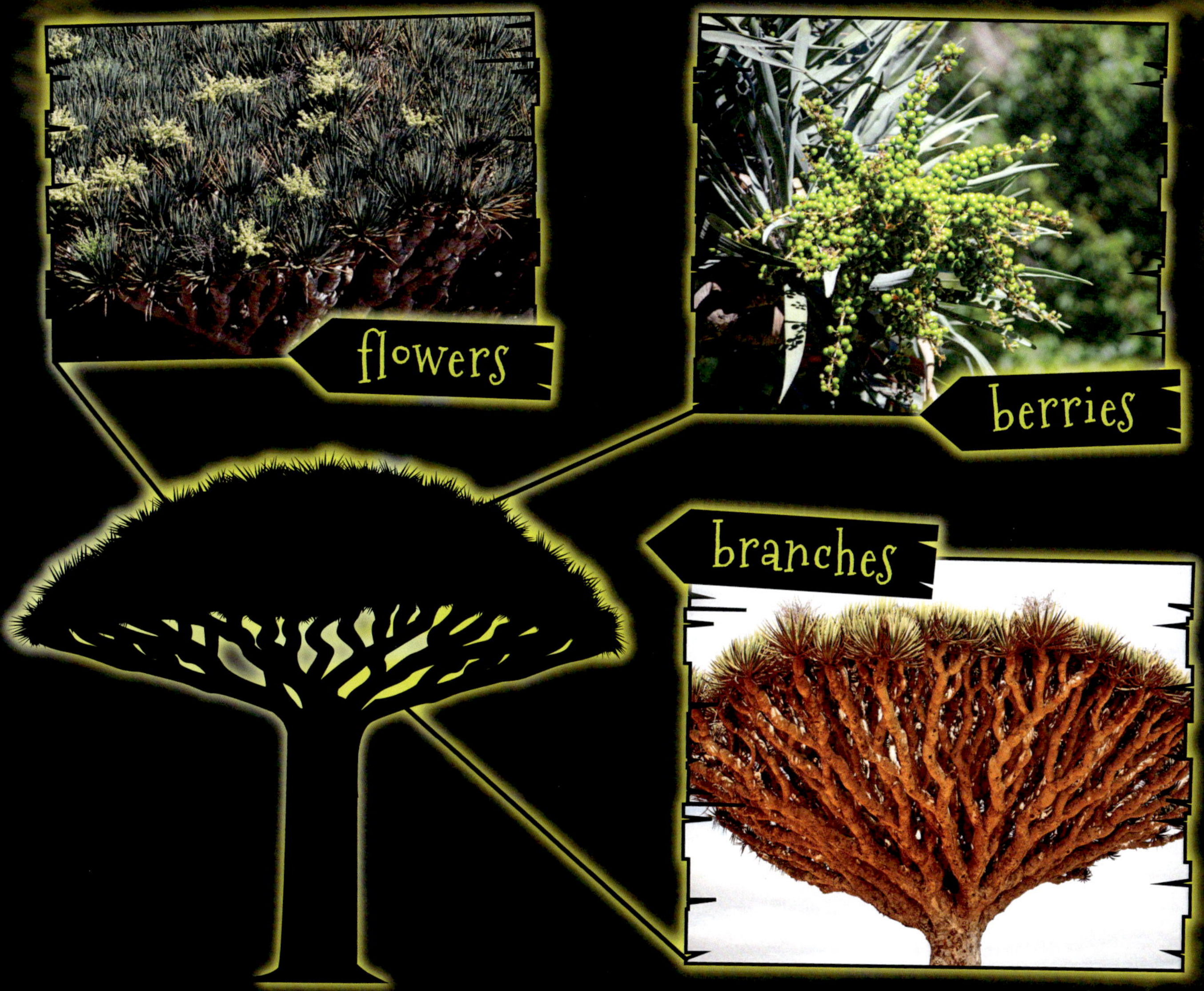

flowers

berries

branches

As the branches of the tree grow, they each separate into two new branches.

AN UNUSUAL SHAPE

Because of the way the dragon's blood tree grows, it looks rather strange. Bare branches reach out and up from the trunk, with leaves clumped together at the tips. The branches have a wavy appearance because of the way they regularly separate into two new branches.

This growth pattern produces a shape that's unlike any tree you're likely used to. People have compared the dragon's blood tree to an umbrella that's been turned inside out or a giant mushroom!

SEEDS OF KNOWLEDGE

The leaves of the dragon's blood tree are quite large. They can be up to 24 inches (60 cm) long.

Scientists can tell how old a dragon's blood tree is by counting the number of times the branches have split from the trunk.

BENEFITS OF ITS BUILD

The weird shape of the dragon's blood tree has benefits. When water collects on the leaves, the tree's shape helps the water flow down to the branches. Then, the water runs down the trunk to the roots. That's pretty clever!

The tree's shape also provides good shade. This prevents the **evaporation** of water from the ground and shades the tree's roots. In addition, the shade gives seedlings, or baby trees, a better chance to grow than they would have in full sun.

SEEDS OF KNOWLEDGE

Since seedlings grow well in the shade of a grown tree, dragon's blood trees often grow close together.

Dragon's blood trees capture water from low, misty clouds.
shade

What Exactly Is Dragon's Blood?

At the beginning of this book, you read that this tree seems to bleed when it's hurt. So what exactly is this "dragon's blood" that comes from this tree?

"Dragon's blood" is actually a resin (REHZ-in). Resin is sticky liquid that flows out of a tree when its bark has been cut. Many trees produce resins. But usually they're yellow or brown. What makes this resin so unusual is its color: dark red. And that's also what gives the tree its name.

Seeds of Knowledge

The people of the island of Socotra call dragon's blood resin "emzoloh."

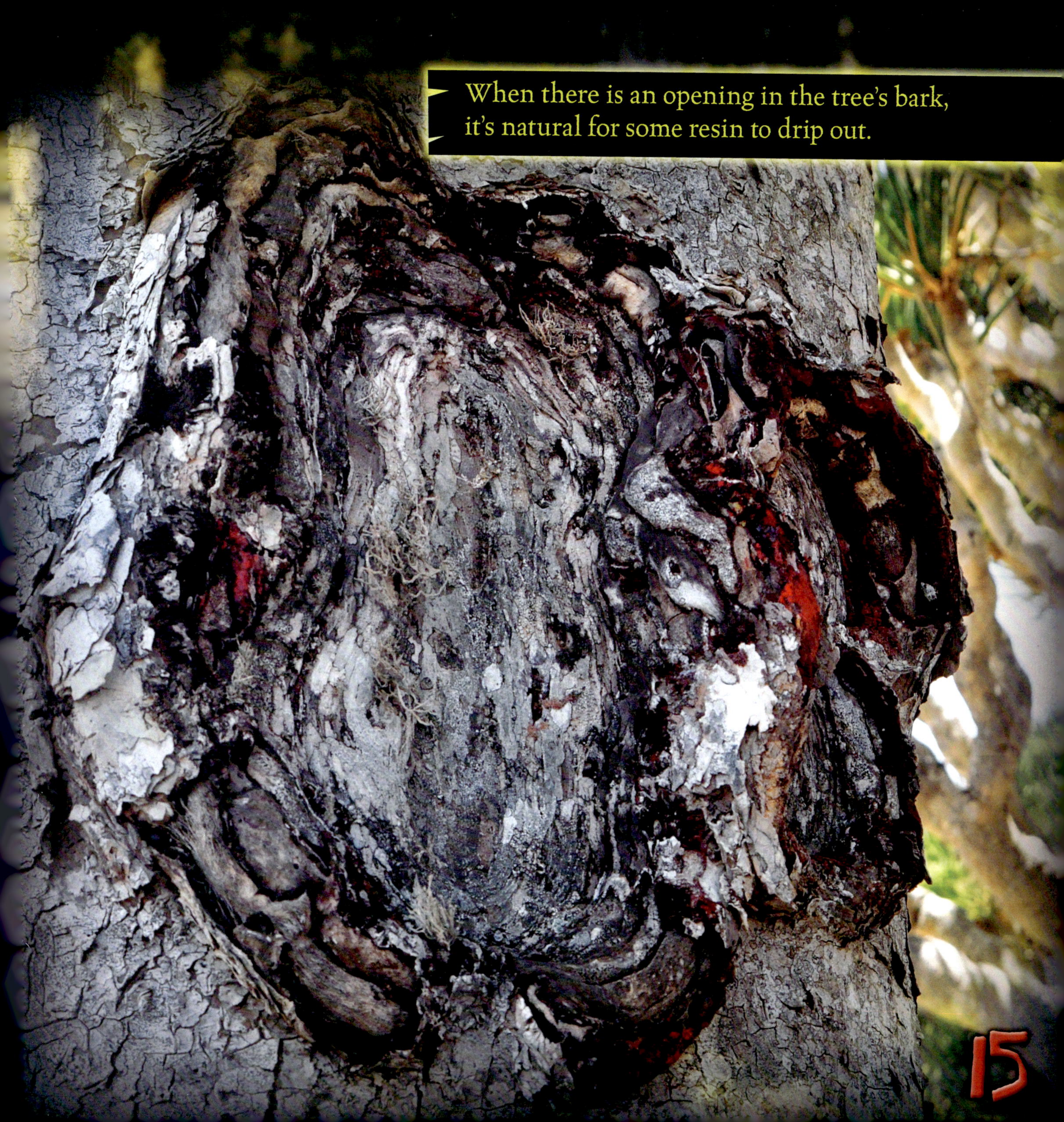

When there is an opening in the tree's bark, it's natural for some resin to drip out.

DRAGON'S BLOOD AS A DRUG

Would you ever think to use tree resin as **medicine**? The people of Socotra did. They've long used the resin of the dragon's blood tree as medicine. They believe it has many useful healing properties.

The resin is commonly used to help heal wounds. It's used to bring down **fevers** and as a blood thinner. It's used to treat **diarrhea** and fight viruses. It's used to treat **muscle** tightness and pain. It's even used to treat the terrible sickness called cancer!

tree resin

People collect the resin from dragon's blood trees using big knives and bowls. Then, it's dried and pounded into powder.

OTHER BENEFITS OF DRAGON'S BLOOD

But wait—there's more! You may have thought it was pretty amazing the dragon's blood tree resin could have so many uses as medicine. But it has many more uses as well.

The resin is used as dye for wool and as paint. It's used as **varnish** for furniture and violins, which are musical instruments with strings. It's used to decorate pots. It's used in beauty supplies. It has even been used in magic. That's a big list of uses!

SEEDS OF KNOWLEDGE

Small amounts of the berries of dragon's blood trees are fed to cows and goats to improve their health. Too many berries will make them sick, though.

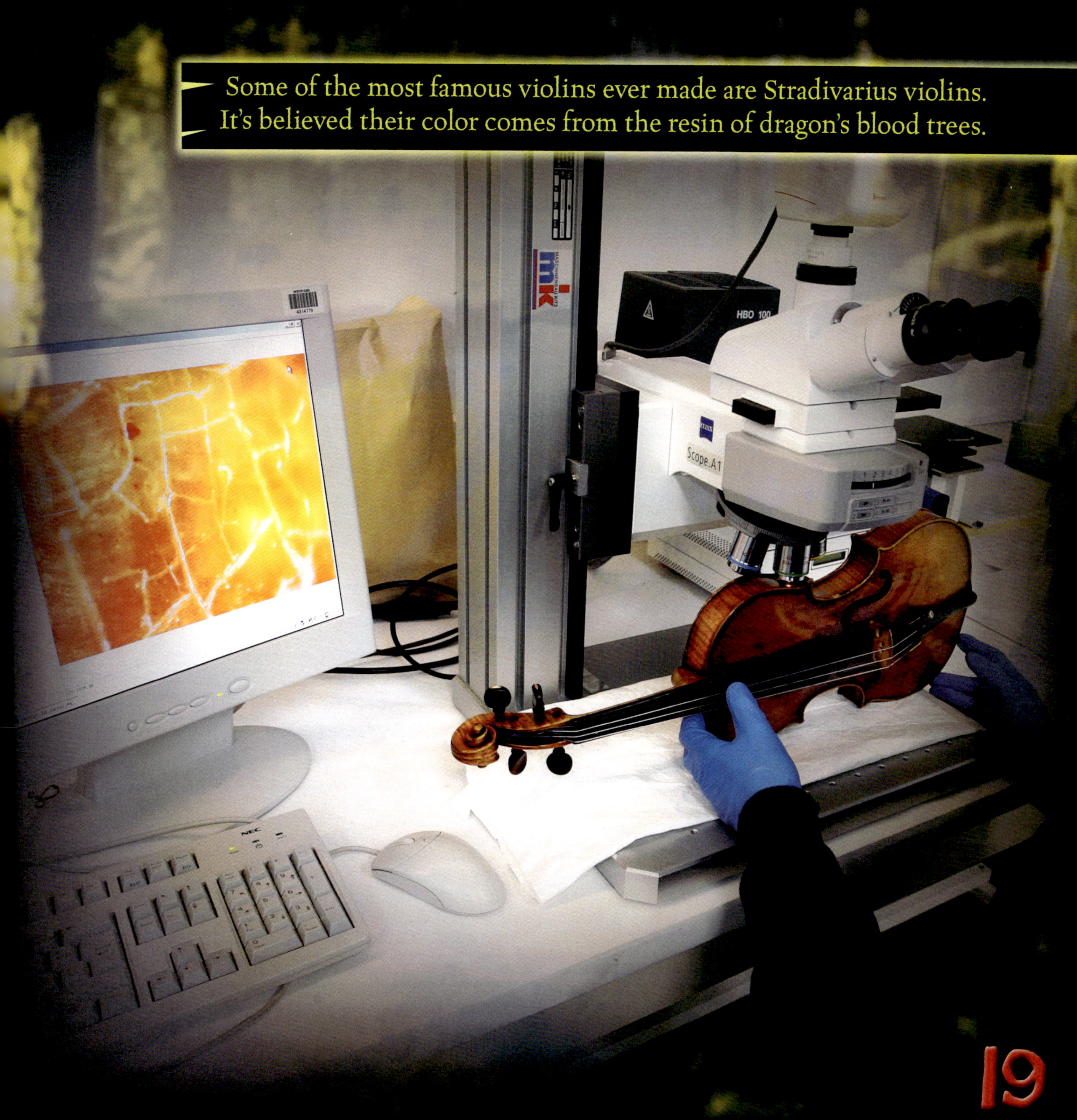

Some of the most famous violins ever made are Stradivarius violins. It's believed their color comes from the resin of dragon's blood trees.

DRAGON'S BLOOD TREES IN DANGER

Sadly, this weird and special tree is in danger. There are many reasons for this. The population of Socotra is growing, and more people are visiting the island. More people means more building is taking place. This has broken up the **habitat** of the dragon's blood tree.

Partly due to **climate change**, Socotra is becoming drier, and the monsoon the trees need doesn't come as regularly. Already, fewer new seedlings are appearing. It's possible this wonderful tree could disappear forever!

SEEDS OF KNOWLEDGE

In some places, the young trees don't look like regular dragon's blood trees. They have tall trunks that don't branch out to form the usual shape of an inside-out umbrella or giant mushroom.

Some believe the dragon's blood tree could lose almost half of its habitat by 2080.

GLOSSARY

climate change: long-term change in Earth's climate, caused partly by human activities such as burning oil and natural gas

cycle: a series of events that happens over and over again

diarrhea: very soft or runny solid waste from a person or animal

evaporation: the act of changing from a liquid into a gas

fever: a body temperature that is higher than normal

habitat: the natural place where an animal or plant lives

medicine: a drug taken to make a sick person well

monsoon: a seasonal change in wind direction resulting in a change in rainfall

muscle: one of the parts of the body that allow movement

plateau: a large area of land with raised sides and a level top

trunk: the thick main stem of a tree

varnish: a liquid that is spread on a surface and that dries to form a hard, shiny coating

For More Information

Books

Gifford, Clive. *Unusual Wonders.* London, United Kingdom: Wayland, 2018.

Lawrence, Ellen. *Extreme Trees: And How They Got That Way.* New York, NY: Bearport Publishing Company, 2015.

Loh-Hagan, Virginia. *Weird Nature.* Ann Arbor, MI: 45th Parallel Press, 2018.

Websites

Dragon Blood Tree
easyscienceforkids.com/dragon-blood-tree/
Learn more about dragon's blood trees on this site.

Dragon Blood Tree Facts
www.softschools.com/facts/plants/dragon_blood_tree_facts/2718/
Discover interesting facts about dragon's blood trees on this website.

See the Unique and Endangered Dragon's Blood Trees of Socotra
www.nationalgeographic.co.uk/video/tv/see-unique-and-endangered-dragons-blood-trees-socotra
Watch a video about dragon's blood trees here and learn about the dangers they face.

Publisher's note to educators and parents: Our editors have carefully reviewed these websites to ensure that they are suitable for students. Many websites change frequently, however, and we cannot guarantee that a site's future contents will continue to meet our high standards of quality and educational value. Be advised that students should be closely supervised whenever they access the Internet.

INDEX